Special / Novelty

D1238293

HEY SENSEI!

Copyright © 2022 by Kris Wilder and Lawrence A. Kane

Illustrations by Kris Wilder

Cover design and interior layout by Kami Miller

All rights reserved. No part of this publication may be reproduced, distributed or transmitted in any form or by any means, including photocopying, recording, or other electronic or mechanical methods, without the prior written permission of the publisher, except in the case of brief quotations embodied in critical reviews and certain other noncommercial uses permitted by copyright law. For permission requests, contact Stickman Publications through our website (www.stickmanpublications.com), email Lawrence Kane (lakane@ix.netcom.com) or Kris Wilder (kriswilder@kriswilder.com), or write to the publisher, addressed "Attention: Permissions Coordinator," at the address below:

Stickman Publications, Inc.
Seattle, WA 98126
www.stickmanpublications.com

ISBN-13: 979-8-9855617-4-6

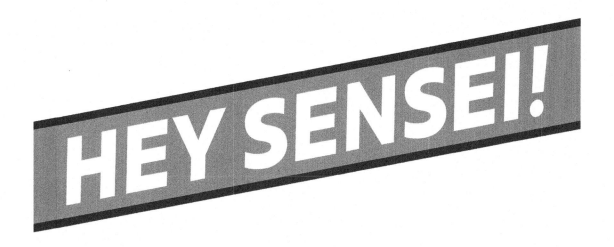

HEY SENSEI!

Funny and Sometimes Insightful
Things That Happened at the Dojo

KRIS WILDER with **LAWRENCE A. KANE**

There is an inherent joy in teaching martial arts to children, an enchantment you will find reflected here. In reading this book you will smile, even laugh. As a martial artist of any tenure, you will declare, "Yes! That really happened!" Although the words you read may not match your exact experience, the emotions certainly will...

Several years ago, while chuckling about a kooky comment thrown out by an eight-year-old, a parent observed, "You should write that down." We did. And we added illustrations to some of them too. These drawings are admittedly unpolished, yet that unsophisticated effect lends itself to the tone of this book. Kids are unpolished too.

Some of these images were originally pinned on the *dojo* corkboard, taped to the waiting area wall, or posted on social media. Over time these vignettes grew in number and distinction, eventually evolving into this book.

Although fun, the contents are based on the traditional values inherent in a well-run martial arts school. *Dojo kun* (principles) vary, yet the concepts of respect, diligence, good manners, big spirit, and the like are ubiquitous and well known. In fact, kids who excel in martial arts often go on to earn varsity sports accolades, National Honor Society memberships, elected offices, leadership roles in business or academia, and more... and as instructors we are fondly able to reflect upon our small role in enabling our students' accomplishments.

Having spent time training for kids you will nod your head knowingly at the moments captured here. As a student, you will be able to say, "Hey, I remember..."

As instructors, we all too often encounter kids who are doing their level best to keep their heads above water. These kids face challenges that in a fair and just world no child should have to deal with. For example, we had a nine-year-old student who was trying his best to keep his compromised grandfather's home in order. Having been abandoned by his mother, and never having met his father, his grandfather who was struggling with late-stage dementia was his whole world, that child's sole source of family, food, trust, and shelter.

Even in an unfair world, children who study martial arts learn the value of merit. After an examination, a student might say, "Thank you for giving me my belt," while instructors reply, "You earned it." With competency-based instruction we help youngsters discover pride in their accomplishments, learn the ability to set and achieve meaningful goals, and then set them up to leverage that proficiency for personal and professional growth for the rest of their lives.

You see, respect for oneself and others is an important link to growing into a mature adult, becoming a productive citizen. This vital life lesson begins in the kid's classes; Little Dragons, Tiny Tigers, or whatever we call them, these are the names for the container that holds the gold... and it is carried with our students far beyond the training hall.

The joy that these children put back into the world can be contagious. Comments, quips, acts of innocence, even the proudly displayed hole in one's gums where a tooth once was, it's all part of the package. More often than not it's a joyous package, metaphorically wrapped in a bow of happiness, though as of this writing Kris found two used band-aids on the mat over two consecutive nights. Sometimes it can be a less-than-perfect too, but that's all part of the experience.

For the most part, these moments are seen, enjoyed, and subsequently lost in the succeeding moments of the training unless we take active steps to jot them down or commit them to memory. Over the years we have tried to capture these moments in illustrations and witticisms that you can enjoy, laugh at, and fondly remember.

Yours in *budo*,

Kris & Lawrence

P.S. If you want to have fun, cut a page or two from this book and post them at your martial arts school. You will be surprised by the energy, laughter, and sometimes challenges it creates for your students.

IT HAPPENED AT THE DOJO

Calvin stepped on a nail and still came to class

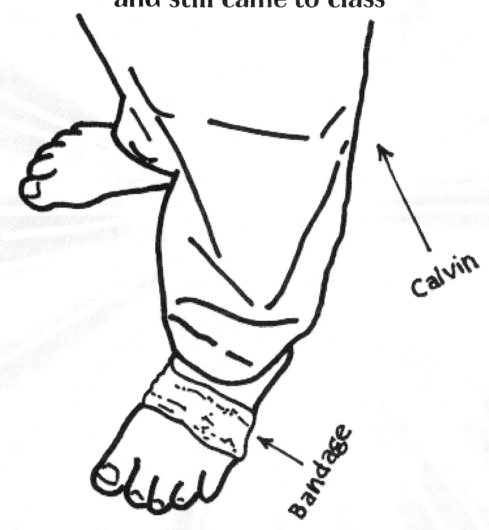

SAID AT THE DOJO

"That happens again we
are all doing push-ups
on broken glass."

"Sensei, we can
do them at my
house I have lots
of broken glass!"

"You have to move or I WILL punch you!"

"All right I'm going to turn on the fans; you deserve some oxygen."

IT HAPPENED AT THE DOJO

Keys left on the floor under the bench

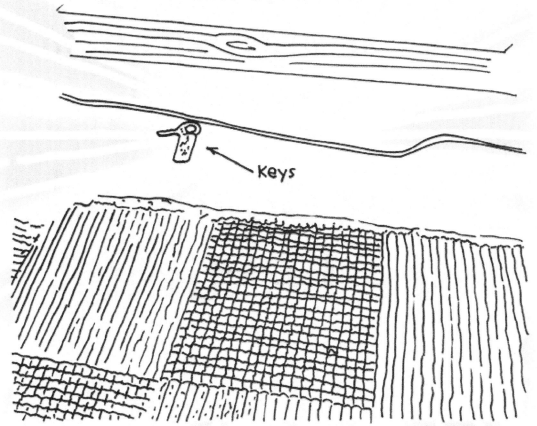

Yelled from the ranks
after another repetition
was called for:

"Don't do a weak one, be strong!"

SAID AT THE DOJO

I said, "You came to the dojo not sitting at home watching Gilligan's Island. Don't waste your time."

"Sensei, Gilligan's Island is a good show. You shouldn't make fun of it."

May I swing the stick to hit people?

IT HAPPENED AT THE DOJO

**Technically in the waiting area,
and just missing the dojo floor**

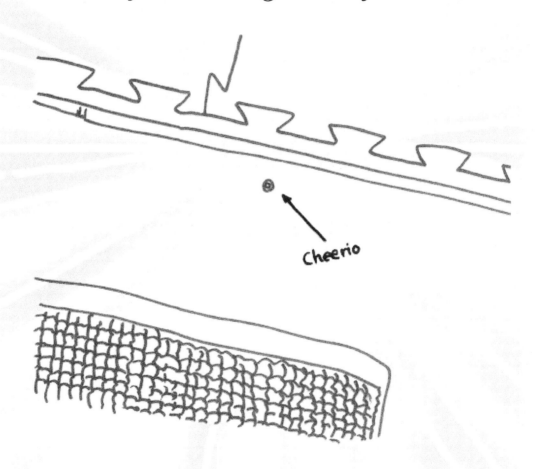

Cheerio

SAID AT THE DOJO

"1, 2, 4,
defend
yourself!"

"In the city of throws, being the craftiest alligator is best"

"My daughter calls you Sensei Wooo!"

I often "Wooo," in class when something good happens.

IT HAPPENED AT THE DOJO

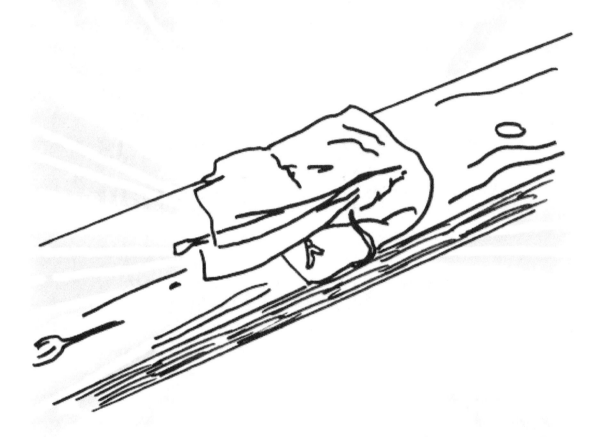

**Leaving your gi at the dojo?
That'll be a few push-ups
before you get that back.**

"Your technique folds like a Kmart lawn chair."

"What's a Kmart?"

"Get loud! You
don't know what
a kiai is?"

"Sure, we got
our couch from
that store."

SAID AT THE DOJO

A five-year-old voice from
the back of the dojo:

"Mistakes are O.K. it means you are working your brain!"

IT HAPPENED AT THE DOJO

Felipe bought this bo to replace the one he broke with his shin. Felipe is 2 years from retirement and has 2 knee replacements. How cool is that?

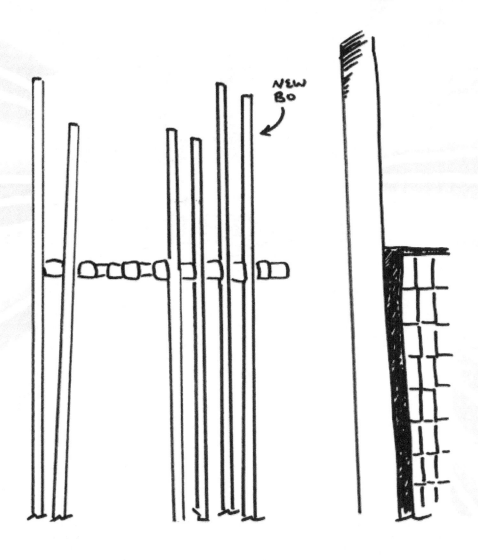

"That was weak, let's do it again!"

yelled a ten-year-old girl
from the front row

"My stiches are out, I took them out myself."

said a seven-year old proudly

SAID AT THE DOJO

"Sorry, did that
hurt you?"

"Only emotionally."

IT HAPPENED AT THE DOJO

What people think the path to Black belt looks like

BLACK BELT

↑

WHITE BELT

What the path to Black belt really looks like

BLACK BELT

WHITE BELT

"Dang, that
was just
cold."

Double elbow bandages from a dog lunging at a squirrel, no excuses karate training to do.

"I'm not gonna give up!"

Out of a mouth of a five-year-old
during a challenge drill.

SAID AT THE DOJO

Student 1.

"That's not the way I saw it on the internet."

Student 2.

"Well, the internet says a lot of things."

SAID AT THE DOJO

"I'm okay, that just got me in the lip."

IT HAPPENED AT THE DOJO

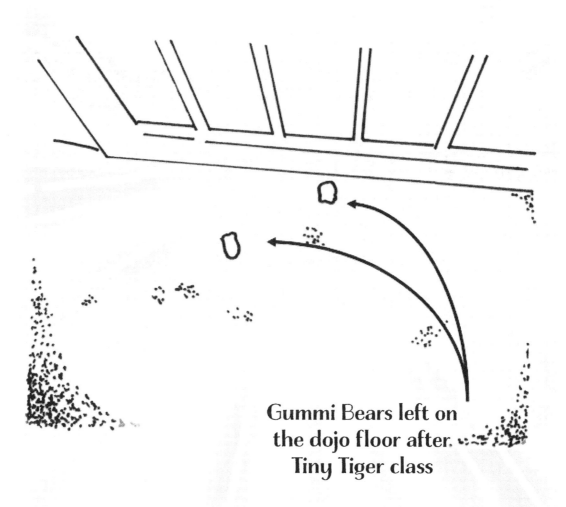

Gummi Bears left on
the dojo floor after
Tiny Tiger class

"I'm the king of push-ups!"

Yelled an eleven-year-old as he jumped up from the floor.

SAID AT THE DOJO

"You kick well."

"Yup. My Mom
says I kicked
her all the time
when I was in
her tummy."

"That makes really good sense Sensei."

(Internal Conversation: I'm glad it is sticking)

Rory Miller uses your dojo for a seminar and the next day you find a piece of skin with some hair attached on the floor.

"My hands are sweaty!"

"Yeah... that's gonna happen."

SAID AT THE DOJO

"Uhm, what are you doing?"

"Got to stretch my bones!"

"Do that
again and
my arm will
go snappy
poo."

IT HAPPENED AT THE DOJO

DATE LINE: After the Tiny Tiger's Class

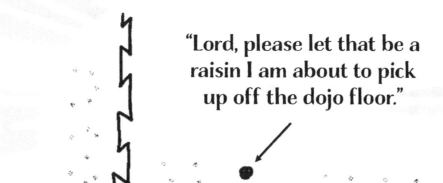

"Lord, please let that be a raisin I am about to pick up off the dojo floor."

"I don't know what that is you just said, but it sounds dangerous. Let's do it."

SAID AT THE DOJO

"Why is your hand on your chest like that?"

"My heart!"

"Your heart is on the other side."

SAID AT THE DOJO

"I need a volunteer."

"Yes, Simon, you volunteer?"

"No, I volunteer Dave."

IT HAPPENED AT THE DOJO

Nigel came to class with a fractured arm

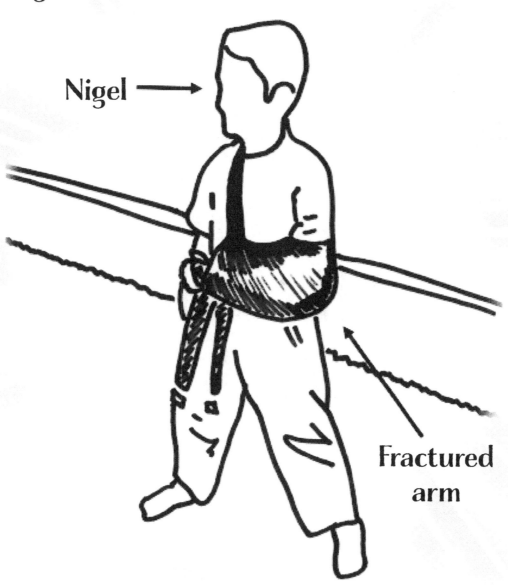

Nigel →

Fractured arm

"Sensei, I threw-up in the restroom. The toilet won't flush."

"That was all Bam Bam & no Pebbles."

(Think The Flintstones)

SAID AT THE DOJO

"Is this a dojo?"

"Yes."

"Huh, it looks like
a Pizza Hut."

IT HAPPENED AT THE DOJO

Dane came to grading with a brown belt and two sleeves on his gi. He left with a black belt and one less sleeve.

Brown belt

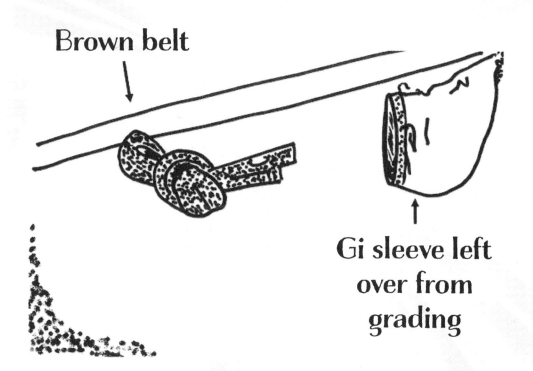

Gi sleeve left over from grading

"You OK?"

"Yeah, the floor got in the way."

Two students having an exchange.

"Was that right?"

"Sorry didn't mean to glare at you."

SAID AT THE DOJO

"This pin is called
kesa gatame."

"A case of salami?"

"Um ... no."

Tucked away in a little gap in the mats on the dojo floor was a Tiny Tiger's used Band-Aid. It was a Captain America Band-Aid.

"What in the world is on your gi?"

"I tried to chug a Slurpee."

"I thought I could do it, but now I immediately regret my decision to volunteer."

"No, I don't know how many I'm doing, I'm just doing."

IT HAPPENED AT THE DOJO

When anybody asks dried
chocolate milk on a gi looks
just like dried blood.

SAID AT THE DOJO

Me: "How's the outside training?"

Tweener: "When my friend gets kata wrong I use a squirt bottle."

Me: "We need to talk."

SAID AT THE DOJO

"What does karate mean?"

Reply from the back of the ranks.

"No joking around and work hard."

SAID AT THE DOJO

"I don't wanna be good, I don't wanna be great, I want to be amazing!"

IT HAPPENED AT THE DOJO

That bruise on Rosie's arm officially came from her trombone at band camp, not the dojo.

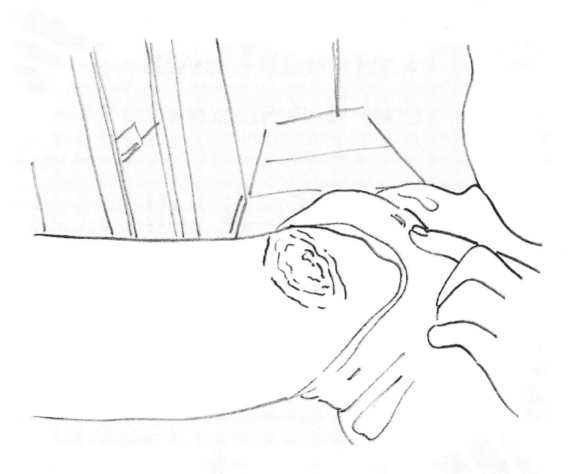

SAID AT THE DOJO

Me: "What is that?
I wouldn't even
call it a stance."

Kid: "Er... I call
it sad dachi?"

SAID AT THE DOJO

Me: "That make sense?"

Kid: "Even a baby with a proper mind sees that."

Me: "Oookay..."

"That's some blood on your sleeve?"

"Oh, it's mostly snot."

SAID AT THE DOJO

No, the fingers should be bent the other way. You know, slightly.

SAID AT THE DOJO

"Is that a rock
on the mat?"

"Oh, that's mine,
thanks."

Kid placing the rock back inside his gi.

"That lock is like a best friend forever, it never lets go!"

SAID AT THE DOJO

Demonstrating a move in
front of the kids class.

"Is your hand
like my hand?"

"Mine smells
different."

IT HAPPENED AT THE DOJO

When you break on of Sensei's bo training. You get to take it home. Nice work Jeramiah.

SAID AT THE DOJO

After a successful examination
in the kid class.

"What do I do with my old belt?"

"Take it home."

"Oh, like a skull from Predator!"

"Break your
fall, not
your face."

SAID AT THE DOJO

From the four-to six-year-old class

"Sensei, my friend David, he's allergic to oranges and farts."

IT HAPPENED AT THE DOJO

She didn't want to miss
class. So she wore her boot
for her sprained ankle.

SAID AT THE DOJO

Upon meeting a new Tiny Tiger

"Sensei, can I headbutt you?"

"Hey, that's my
water bottle under
the bench!"

"Then take it home."

Two weeks later, still there
under the bench

SAID AT THE DOJO

"How are you tonight?"

Kid casually walking past.

"I threw up at school today."

IT HAPPENED AT THE DOJO

A first.

A needle on
the dojo floor.

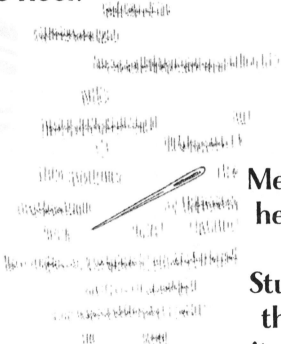

Me: "What the
heck is this?"

Student: "Hey,
that is mine,
it came out of
my pants."

SAID AT THE DOJO

"Hey where you been?"

"I broke my collar bone at camp. I only cried for 5 minutes instead of 20."

SAID AT THE DOJO

"Don't gulp your water like that, you'll throw-up."

"It's okay, I only throw-up a little."

"I'm taking you down...

from the inside."

IT HAPPENED AT THE DOJO

This is Scarlett.
She is 5 years old
and does push-ups
like a Marine Corp.
Lance Corporal!

Look out world
she's heading
your way.

SAID AT THE DOJO

"Why are
you holding
your ears?"

"You said, keep
your hands up."

"Why are you so happy at these exercises?"

"Cuz I'm an excellent student!"

"Sensei, that thing you said, it sounds like a wise thing from a T.V. show."

IT HAPPENED AT THE DOJO

Yes-Pep's cast for her broken arm makes for a painful head block.

"Sensei, it took a week but I did 1000 punches at home!"

Excellent...

Me: "Are you waving at your training partner?"

Student: "The Bruce Lee wave, you know, come get some."

Student: "This is not convenient."

Me: "No. No it's not."

IT HAPPENED AT THE DOJO

Ella came straight from school no Gi.
Good choice. Extra effort at school,
still made the dojo that night.

SAID AT THE DOJO

"Time for
fundamentals."

"Sensei, you mean
FUN-damentals."

"Yes I do!"

"I threaten you with push-ups and now you do it right?"

"Yeah. Threats work."

"You gonna keep coming at me with play money?"

IT HAPPENED AT THE DOJO

Bit by a rabbit (she claims
it was a bunny)
Lilly still showed up to train

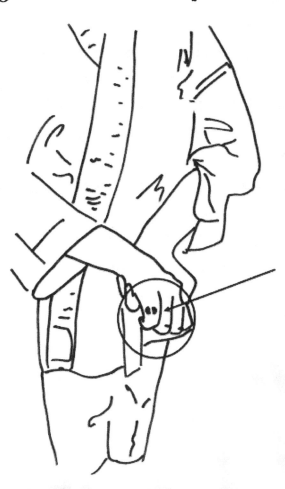

"What in the world
are you doing?"

"I don't know what
my body does!"

SAID AT THE DOJO

Me: "It's not hard we're only doing this for 60 seconds."

Kid: "Ahhh, why not a full minute?"

SAID AT THE DOJO

Me: "There is no such thing as muscle memory."

Kid: "Sure until they turn on us."

IT HAPPENED AT THE DOJO

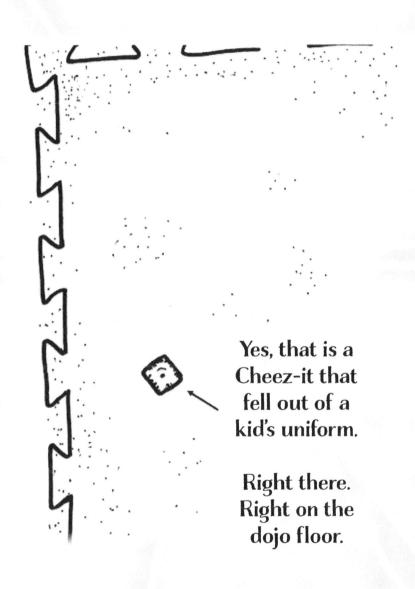

Yes, that is a Cheez-it that fell out of a kid's uniform.

Right there. Right on the dojo floor.

SAID AT THE DOJO

Me: "Good you balanced that for five seconds!"

Kid: "Uh, Sensei, five-and-a-half seconds."

Me: "You're excited class is over."

Kid: "Yeah, it's Taco Tuesday, tacos for dinner!"

"Kata is like a sandwich it has a beginning a middle and an end."

"I like sandwiches!"

IT HAPPENED AT THE DOJO

Knee to nose.

Pep kicked so high and hard she gave herself a bloody nose.

Well...gotta respect the effort.

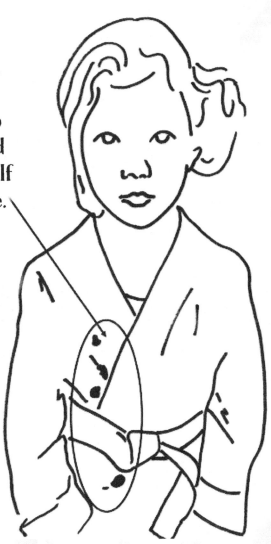

SAID AT THE DOJO

"That's a
sloppy dog."

"A what?"

"A lousy technique."

IT HAPPENED AT THE DOJO

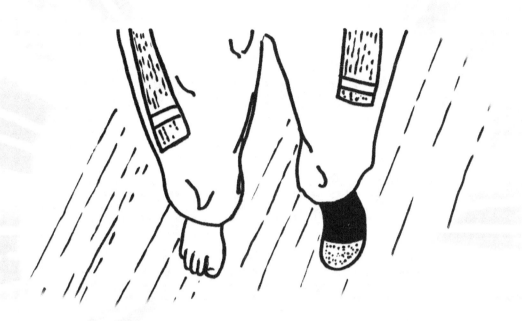

Sensei, you remember that
nail I stepped on at home?

I found a new one.

"Be like butter."

"Didn't you mean be like water?"

IT HAPPENED AT THE DOJO

Kate got on the Makiwara
the other night. Working
hard and learning.

"Well, if you're asking, a donut with sprinkles. It's more sugar."

"Tearing off your skin is not an exercise."

SAID AT THE DOJO

Me: "What's your
favorite class
in school?"

Kid: "Math. Math
and fire."

IT HAPPENED AT THE DOJO

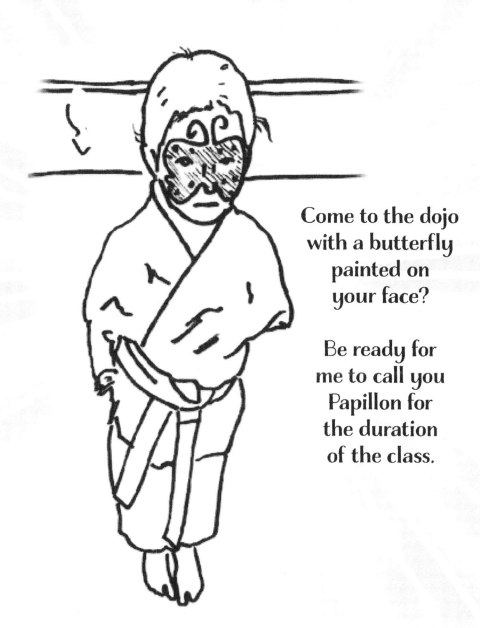

Come to the dojo
with a butterfly
painted on
your face?

Be ready for
me to call you
Papillon for
the duration
of the class.

"Why gravity, why!"

SAID AT THE DOJO

A five-year-old voice from
the back of the dojo

"If you give up, you don't get better."

"Sorry, didn't mean to hurt you."

"Pain is my middle name."

IT HAPPENED AT THE DOJO

Not part of any kata,
but impressive.

SAID AT THE DOJO

Overheard between two kids.

"I wish my name was Machete Ninja Star."

"Do you have some equipment like this at home?"

"No. And if we did it would be broken by now."

"Should we do a kata we know?"

"What other kata would we do?"

IT HAPPENED AT THE DOJO

Can't disagree with what this student
had written on the back of his hand.

"Did I mention Alec got all A's at school?"

"About 6 times..."

"Get ready for 7."

SAID AT THE DOJO

"Don't do that, it's for the kids class."

"I want to hold on to my childhood as long as I can."

– Overheard –

"Sorry, did that hurt?"

"A new level of pain, but no."

IT HAPPENED AT THE DOJO

It is official.

The 1 Millionth set of
socks left at the dojo.

"No, that's
my brother,
I have a
bigger
head."

"All Play-Doh tastes salty no matter what the color."

"I don't have armpits! Oh, (giggle) I mean armpit hair."

IT HAPPENED AT THE DOJO

Abby hurt her ankle in dance. She came to class-took it easy-but still came to class.

Me: "Why are you standing so close?"

Kid: "You said listen closely."

"Hey is
that a juice
box? A juice
box fixes
everything."

"This drill is like smooth jazz, you can go anywhere with it."

IT HAPPENED AT THE DOJO

After class even the youngest
gets to show of what she learned
from seeing her big brother.

Dragon
shirt

Polka dot
rubber boots

"You Okay?"

"Yeah, just a little mucus came up."

"That technique was golden brown, crispy!"

"That karate bunkai looks like angry salsa dancing."

IT HAPPENED AT THE DOJO

A yardstick for measuring

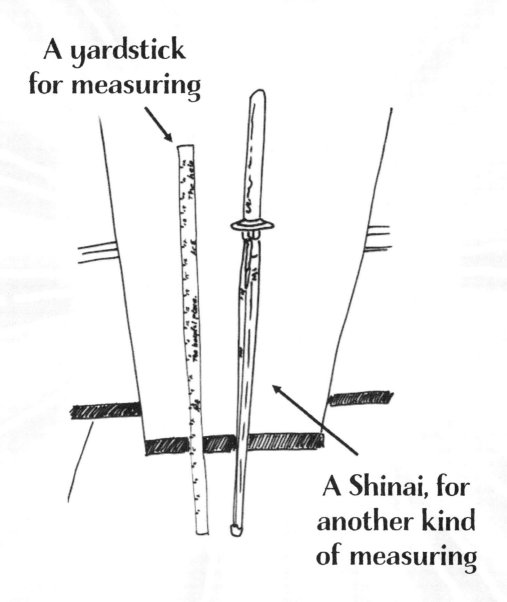

A Shinai, for another kind of measuring

Me: "You've been gone from class."

Student: "Yeah, I fell off a mountain."

SAID AT THE DOJO

"Sensei look at me!"

"I see you."

"Good. I need
the approval."

Overheard during an application training one student to another

"Now, for the big reveal."

IT HAPPENED AT THE DOJO

Omar decided to demonstrate
his Ultimate Self-Defense

SAID AT THE DOJO

Overheard during an application training one student to another

"Nope, not today Mister."

SAID AT THE DOJO

"Would you act like that if your Dad were here?"

Long Pause

"Yeah...I probably would."

SAID AT THE DOJO

From the Tiny Tiger Class

Me: "You're smart."

Student: "It's because we take naps."

IT HAPPENED AT THE DOJO

Kate sprained her finger at school.
Came to class. Did kata. No problem.

SAID AT THE DOJO

"Nice scab you're picking."

Said in a condescending tone

"Yeah I know! I have a bigger on on my side."

SAID AT THE DOJO

"I got his eye!"

"You talk a lot."

"Yup, my brain
goes all the way
to my mouth."

IT HAPPENED AT THE DOJO

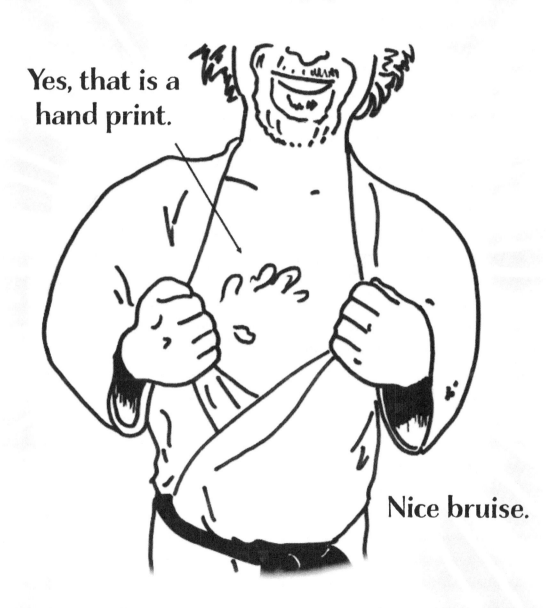

"Be careful,
I had a bad
hair day."

SAID AT THE DOJO

Student after a successful nerve pinch

"Yee-haw! Burn baby burn!"

SAID AT THE DOJO

Student after a competition

"I don't care if I won a medal. Getting better every day is the important to me."

IT HAPPENED AT THE DOJO

When you back-up from a charge swiftly
sometimes the wall pays the price.

Hole

SAID AT THE DOJO

One kid watching another kid do kata

"Ummmm yeah... That kata, we need to fix that."

"My nose only bled twice yesterday."

"Hey Sensei I practiced my kata on the toilet!"

IT HAPPENED AT THE DOJO

Sometimes Dad needs a little help.

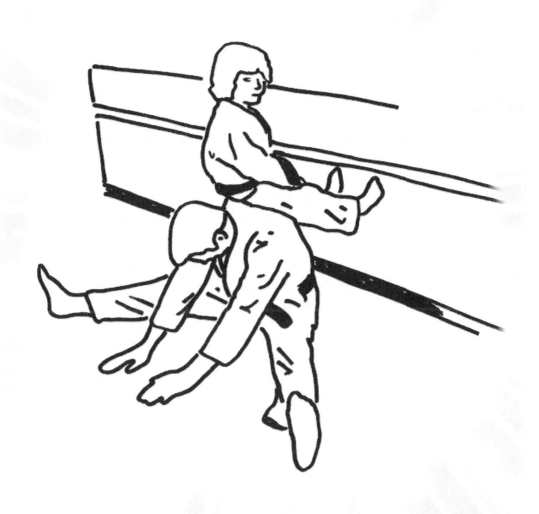

"My mask gets sucked into my nose during sanchin practice."

SAID AT THE DOJO

"Sensei are you going to come see me when I am on Ninja Warrior?"

"Absolutely!"

SAID AT THE DOJO

"Great job on the
bag tonight!"

"I pretended it was
my brother."

IT HAPPENED AT THE DOJO

One young lady decided a toy
plastic arm shield underneath
her Gi was a great resolution.

"Sensei I have no
dignity. Would you
buy some of my sister's
Girl Scout cookies?"

"Of course."

SAID AT THE DOJO

"TikTok is my cardio."

"We'll fix that."

SAID AT THE DOJO

"Give me that stick."

"Why?"

"Because it's a stick
and you're a boy."

IT HAPPENED AT THE DOJO

Isaac still working on his rolls.

SAID AT THE DOJO

"Oh, that's going to be Painful."

SAID AT THE DOJO

Yelled from the back of the dojo.

"You can do it, believe in yourself!"

"The legs break the fall, land on your legs!"

IT HAPPENED AT THE DOJO

Summer is here and scabs need cooling off!

"Hey, my knuckles are red. How about you?"

"Please describe the move to the class."

"Umm, unicorn blast?"

SAID AT THE DOJO

A middle school student asked
to demonstrate a technique.

"Step forward and
prove your worth!"

"Hey. Let's relax a little."

"Oh...oh Okay."

IT HAPPENED AT THE DOJO

Noah had little ninja in his uniform that escaped.

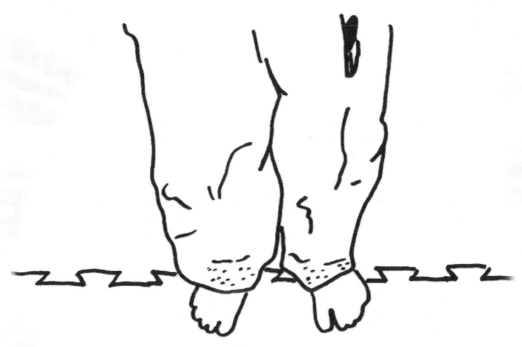

Little plastic ninja will
not be held captive

"Sensei, why do you have a war hammer?"

"It's a chishi."

"Sensei, let's see if I can beat you at push-ups."

"Let's go."

"Sensei
I think
we broke
Nathan."

IT HAPPENED AT THE DOJO

It is November, and you leave your shoes at the Dojo?

"Practice your sanchin breathing."

"Oh you mean casually throwing up?"

"What's your favorite sandwich?

"7."

SAID AT THE DOJO

"My hair sweated!"

IT HAPPENED AT THE DOJO

**Jesse passed his 1st-Kyu.
Next stop Shodan.**

"Oh no, my green belt experience was a lie!"

"Let's do the pretty thing again."

"Let's do sanchin kata."

"You mean, some phlegm kata."

IT HAPPENED AT THE DOJO

Nigel decided a broken arm would be
no deterrent to going to the dojo.

"Sensei you don't have a toenail."

"Ah, yeah let's do some kata."

SAID AT THE DOJO

Said in the Beginning
Kids Class

"Can we break a board on my 8 pack? I have an 8 pack."

"You kids are fast!"

"It's because we have smaller hips."

IT HAPPENED AT THE DOJO

Sensei Felipe passed on his
brown belt from May of 1974 to
a promising young student.

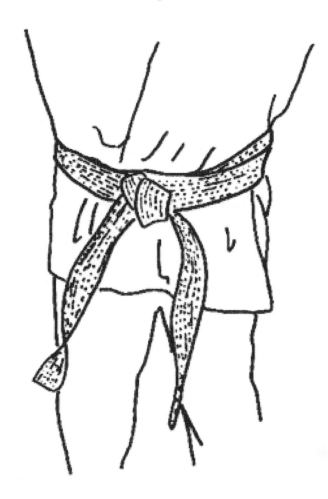

SAID AT THE DOJO

"Sorry I'm late. I got focused on something in the parking lot."

(From a 10 year old. No clarification asked for.)

SAID AT THE DOJO

"Hey Sensei, what's that on the ceiling?"

"Just do your sit-ups please."

"Sensei, I once pried
a Jolly Rancher
candy loose from
the parking lot
and ate it."

IT HAPPENED AT THE DOJO

Lilly stayed after class to
work on her new push-up.

Love that attitude!

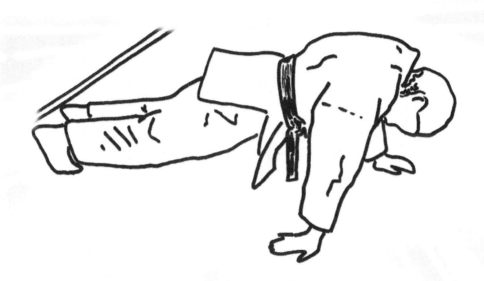

SAID AT THE DOJO

"Everybody is doing it wrong."

"Oh, it's me!"

"Wow, you're on fire!"

"Fire makes it all better."

"My brother threw his red sweatshirt in with the whites."

"Well, that explains the tint of your gi."

IT HAPPENED AT THE DOJO

Josh was working on the bag and
asked specifically for Duct Tape.

"That move is Trans meridian Annihilation!"

"I just made that up..."

SAID AT THE DOJO

"Is that blood
on the mat?"

"Yup, I'll get the
disinfectant."

"You lost a tooth."

"It was loose and I
hit it with my knee
while rolling."

IT HAPPENED AT THE DOJO

Forget your belt.
Welcome to the Belt of Shame

"You're working with a lower rank, don't kill 'em."

"I won't if you don't want me to."

SAID AT THE DOJO

Kid 1: "Why a Mouthguard?"

Kid 2: "So your teeth don't get knocked out."

Kid 1: "Oh, O.K..."

Coolly walking away

"Where's your brother?"

"He's in the car whining."

IT HAPPENED AT THE DOJO

A.J. was in no way going to
let 6 stitches in his chin keep
him from grading night.

He passed.

SAID AT THE DOJO

"Sensei, you watch
YouTube?"

Before I can answer
another kid offers,

"He watches
old man TV."

"When you are using your knuckles don't chuckle."

"First time that technique has been called cute."

"I'm willing to accept that."

IT HAPPENED AT THE DOJO

Two girls had loose teeth. I challenged
them to see who could get their
tooth out first. The competition
was on! Here is your winner.

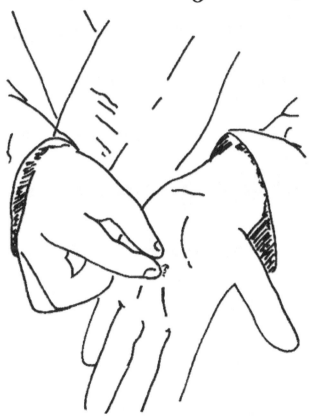

"Wha, what happened?"

"You passed out."

"Doing hard stuff makes your mind grow."

"I think I may have ripped my bones."

IT HAPPENED AT THE DOJO

Yes, that is a Band-Aid left on the Dojo entryway carpet.

"How are you doing on your 1000 kick, 1000 punch challenge?"

"Sensei, I'm in Kindergarten."

"It only takes three days people! I got it done in three days! Apply yourselves!"

"Why are your pants rolled up?"

"You said you wanted to see my knee bend."

IT HAPPENED AT THE DOJO

Yes, you can stop
stretching now.

Show-off.

"When I get my cast off I'm going to make my brother smell my arm."

SAID AT THE DOJO

From the Kids Class

"That is not correct."

"It's OK, I know I'm doing it."

SAID AT THE DOJO

"Why are you
crying?"

"I fell on a cone."

"A safety cone?"

"Yes."

IT HAPPENED AT THE DOJO

Mom has class, so
dinner at the dojo!

"When it (insert disaster) goes down I want you on my team."

"You should know I don't ration well."

"Are you pickin' up what I'm puttin' down?"

"No, I don't know where it's been."

"Sharpen your technique like a sword edge. You understand?"

"Yeah, it means you don't see sundown."

Students making suggestions on what technique to do next.

James, "Would somebody please say, eat tacos!"

"That technique was golden brown and crispy."

SAID AT THE DOJO

"Wow, you are doing better after your test. It must be the belt."

Small voice from the back of the dojo.

"I don't think it's the belt."

"I'm not reflexible."

Said in the Tiny Tigers class

IT HAPPENED AT THE DOJO

SAID AT THE DOJO

"I don't want to be average!"

"What's your favorite food?"

"Cat."

SAID AT THE DOJO

"Do that again and I'm going to eat your gizzard!"

"Go ahead, I don't use that organ."

IT HAPPENED AT THE DOJO

A full day at the pool, two pieces of pizza on the way to the dojo...yup.

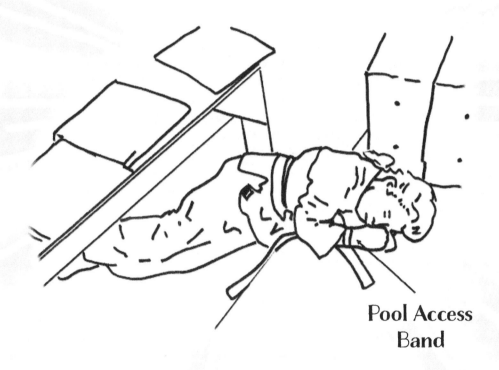

Pool Access
Band

"Step-up and feel the magic."

Said as two students prepare for drills

SAID AT THE DOJO

"Come at me Bro!"

Said in jest

"Wow, this drill is like smooth jazz."

IT HAPPENED AT THE DOJO

Anabel just put some tape on it and kept training. Gotta love that!

SAID AT THE DOJO

"Sensei, I know what responsivity means. I got an iPad and it still isn't broken."

"Stop spinning."

"Oh... not that kind of rotate."

SAID AT THE DOJO

"My son's name
is Reilly."

"He said he wanted
to be called Wally."

"I know, but his name
is really Reilly."

IT HAPPENED AT THE DOJO

**Not the first time a toe got
The Athletic Tape Treatment.**

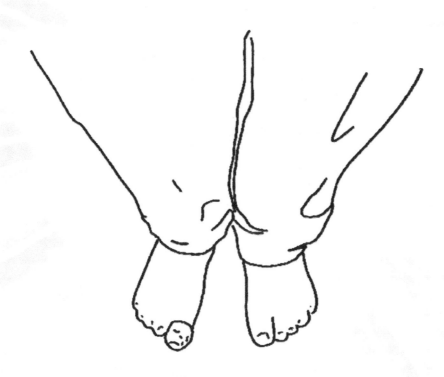

SAID AT THE DOJO

"I have no spine!"

"That's nothing but a storage locker of pain."

Commenting on a karate move

SAID AT THE DOJO

"Sensei I read
your book!"

"Nice, what did
you learn?"

"I dunno that was
like two days ago."

IT HAPPENED AT THE DOJO

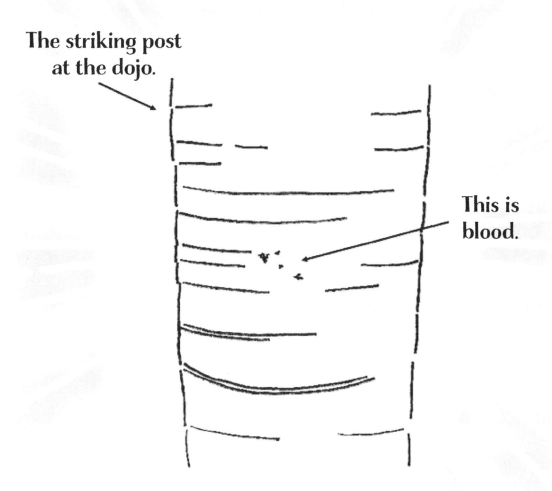

Just out of frame, the bleach...

SAID AT THE DOJO

From the Kids Class

"Do you salute everybody?"

"No just my teachers."

SAID AT THE DOJO

Overheard in the Kids Class

"I'm allergic to stupid."

"His legs are too short. There must be an ointment for that."

IT HAPPENED AT THE DOJO

Behold! Another Band-Aid
on the dojo floor.

"You dirty little cheater."

"Yup."

"Nasty is better than sophisticated."

"This stance makes my legs burn."

"That burning sensation means it's working."

IT HAPPENED AT THE DOJO

Love the, "Can do Attitude."
Just be smart about
getting back on the floor.

SAID AT THE DOJO

"Are you OK?"

"Yeah, I choked on some air."

SAID AT THE DOJO

"Ok everybody, push-ups."

"Can we do one-armed push-ups?"

"Absolutely!"

SAID AT THE DOJO

"Do I get a stripe
on my belt?"

"No, you don't get
anything here,
you earn it."

IT HAPPENED AT THE DOJO

Behold! Another Band-Aid on the dojo floor.
(Technically the entryway carpet)

"You said, 'Do 100 kicks,' so I did 150."

"Sorry I am late for class. I stayed after school to take a test. I got an A."

(Excellent choice)

"The book you recommended, Meditations, by Marcus Aurelius... Wow!"

IT HAPPENED AT THE DOJO

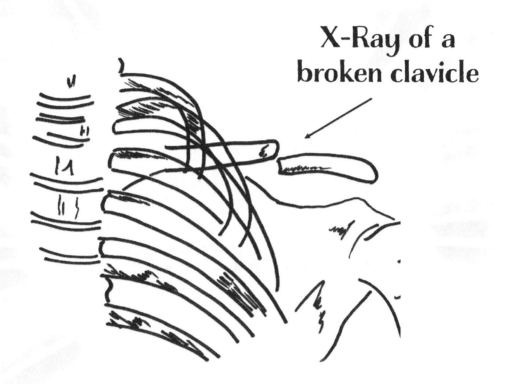

X-Ray of a
broken clavicle

3 weeks after a broken collar bone
Liam showed up for the next rank
examination–and passed.

"I love challenges."

"Sensei is right
you can do karate
when you are old,
look at him."

"Be smooth and cool."

IT HAPPENED AT THE DOJO

Yes, that really happened

SAID AT THE DOJO

"How did you get that scab on your hand?"

"Working on the bag at home."

SAID AT THE DOJO

"Sensei you have
a booger."

"What?"

"I'm little, I can see
up your nose."

"This exercise works the abs."

"I only have a 2 pack to work with."

IT HAPPENED AT THE DOJO

No matter what is said,
no matter how many times,

the discarded Band-Aid
on the dojo floor.

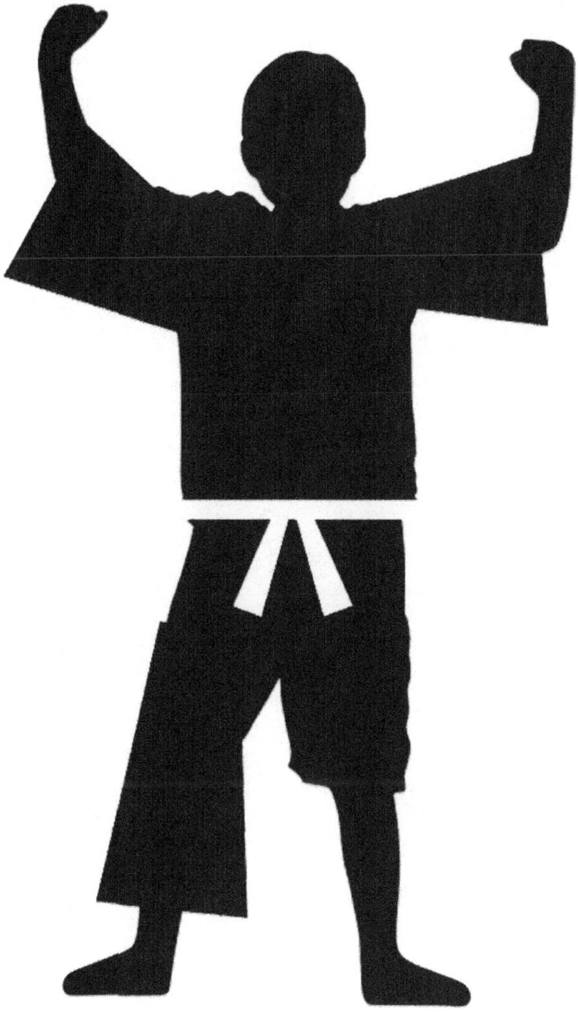

Kris Wilder

Kris was inducted into the United States Martial Arts Hall of Fame in 2018. He began teaching martial arts in 1982 and has seen a lot happen on the training hall floor. He is also the author of numerous books on martial arts and self-improvement. Humor and laughter are the greatest joys in life for people, and the training hall is not exempt from such a treasure. Kris sees stand-up comedy as a brilliant art form and points to Norm MacDonald as his favorite comedian of all time. To further distort his youth, he grew up watching *Monty Python's Flying Circus* and *Fawlty Towers*.

Lawrence Kane

A bestselling author, Lawrence was once interviewed in English by a reporter from a Swiss magazine for an article that was published in French, and finds that oddly amusing. He was inducted into SIG Sourcing Supernova Hall of Fame in 2018. In 2022, he was honored with a Top DEIB Leader Walk the Walk Award. Lawrence has been studying and teaching martial arts since 1970. His quirky sense of humor is tickled by shows like *The Simpsons*, *Monty Python's Flying Circus*, and *Disenchanted*.

Suggested books by the authors to up your game and help others (all available on Amazon):

Dude, The World's Gonna Punch You in the Face (Wilder/Kane)

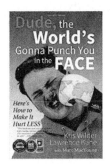

"As an emergency room physician, I see a lot of injuries. This book can save you a lot of pain and trauma, not just physical but also emotional and financial as well." – **Jeff Cooper**, MD

We only get one shot at life. And, it's really easy to screw that up because the world wants to punch us all in the face. Hard! But, what if you knew when to duck? What if you were warned about the dangers—and possibilities—ahead of time? Here is how to man-up and take on whatever the world throws at you. This powerful book arms young men with knowledge about love, wealth, education, faith, government, leadership, work, relationships, life, and violence. It won't prevent all mistakes, nothing will, but it can keep you from making the impactful ones that you'll regret the most. This book is quick knowledge, easy to read, and brutally frank, just the way the world gives it to you, except without the pain. Read on. Learn how to see the bad things coming and avoid them.

The Way of Martial Arts for Kids (Wilder)

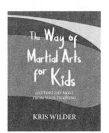

"Written in a personable, engaging style that will appeal to kids and adults alike." – **Laura Weller**, Guitarist, *The Green Pajamas*

Based on centuries of traditions, martial arts training can be a positive experience for kids. The book helps you and yours get the most out of every class. It shows how just about any child can become one of those few exemplary learners who excel in the training hall as well as in life. Written to children, it is also for parents as well. After all, while the martial arts instructor knows his art, no one knows his/her child better than the parent. Together you can help your child achieve just about anything... The advice provided is straightforward, easy to understand, and written with a child-reader in mind so that it can either be studied by the child and/or read together with the parent to assure solid results.

10 Rules of Karate (Wilder/Kane)

"Since losing isn't an option on or off the mat, this is an absolute must read for karateka." – **Christian Wedewardt**, Founder & Head of Karatepraxis

All ten precepts in this concise book cut to the heart of ending physical confrontations as quickly as possible with empty-hand techniques. Our definition of "ending" is to make the attack stop. There is no running after the now fleeing assailant to catch and strike him down. There is no lesson, no teaching, no therapy, no epiphany. There is only making that bad guy stop what he is doing instantly so that you and those you care about will be safe. These ten principles are style agnostic, all about ending fights immediately. They define how to best apply your skills and training in the real world. Those who work with these principles will find swiftness, clarity, and victory in so doing.

Musashi's Dokkodo (Kane/Wilder)

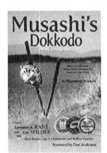

"The authors have made classic samurai wisdom accessible to the modern martial artist like never before!" – **Goran Powell**, award winning author of *Chojun* and *A Sudden Dawn*

Shortly before he died, Miyamoto Musashi (1584 – 1645) wrote down his final thoughts about life for his favorite student Terao Magonojō to whom *Go Rin No Sho*, his famous *Book of Five Rings*, had also been dedicated. He called this treatise *Dokkodo*, which translates as *"The Way of Walking Alone."* This treatise contains Musashi's original 21 precepts of the *Dokkodo* along with five different interpretations of each passage written from the viewpoints of a monk, a warrior, a teacher, an insurance executive, and a businessman. In this fashion you are not just reading a simple translation of Musashi's writing, you are scrutinizing his final words for deeper meaning. In them are enduring lessons for how to lead a successful and meaningful life.

Sh!t Sun Tzu Said (Kane/Wilder)

"If you had to choose one variant of Sun Tzu's collected work, this one should be at the top of the pile... I loved it!" – **Jeffrey-Peter Hauck**, MSc, JD, Police SGT (Ret.), LPI, CPT USA, Professor of Criminal Justice

Sun Tzu was a famous Chinese general whose mastery of strategy was so exceptional that he reportedly transformed 180 courtesans into skilled soldiers in a single training session. While that episode was likely exaggerated, historians agree that Sun Tzu defeated the Ch'u, Qi, and Chin states for King Ho-Lu, forging his empire. In 510 BC, Master Tzu recorded his winning strategies in Art of War, the earliest surviving and most revered tome of its kind. With methods so powerful they can conquer an adversary's spirit, you can use Master Tzu's strategies to overcome any challenge, from warfare to self-defense to business negotiations. This book starts with the classic 1910 translation of *Art of War*, adds modern and historical insight, and demonstrates how to put the master's timeless wisdom to use in your everyday life. In this fashion, the *Art of War* becomes accessible for the modern mind, simultaneously entertaining, enlightening, and practical.

Made in the USA
Monee, IL
08 February 2023

26851345R00155